NBA CHAMPIONSHIPS:

↓

1991, 1992, 1993, 1996, 1997, 1998

↓

ALL-TIME LEADING SCORER:

↓

MICHAEL JORDAN (1984–93, 1995–98):

↓

29,277 POINTS

CONTENTS

Rising above the shores of Lake Michigan, the **CHICAGO** skyline is one of the nation's most recognizable.

THE BIRTH OF THE BULLS

The Chicago Bulls clung to a one-point lead over the Cleveland Cavaliers. It was May 7, 1989, the deciding game of the first playoff round of the National Basketball Association (NBA). The Bulls were

Chicago Packers scoring sensation **WALT BELLAMY** faced Wilt Chamberlain in 1962.

underdogs. The Cavs had finished far ahead of them in the standings. With just a few seconds left, Cleveland's Craig Ehlo scored on a layup. Now the Cavaliers led by a point. The Bulls' Michael Jordan took the inbound pass near center court. He dribbled toward the foul line. With one second left, he leaped for a jump shot. He seemed to suspend himself in midair as Ehlo flew past him. Then he let go of the ball. Nothing but net! Chicago won 101–100! Jordan's jump for joy after sinking the shot became famous. Since then, his game-winner has been known simply as "The Shot." Chicago eventually bowed out of the playoffs. But the game showed that the Bulls were about to become one of the NBA's best.

The Bulls weren't the first professional basketball team in the "Windy City." The Chicago Stags played four years between 1946 and 1950. The Chicago Packers began playing in 1961. They lost 62 games. Fans

LEGENDS OF THE HARDWOOD

LOCAL GUYS MAKE GOOD

JOHNNY KERR, COACH, 6-FOOT-9, 1966–68
JERRY SLOAN, GUARD/FORWARD, 6-FOOT-5, 1966–76

In high school, Johnny Kerr played soccer. After growing eight inches, he turned to basketball. He played for the University of Illinois. The Fighting Illini advanced to the NCAA Final Four in 1952. Later, he helped the Syracuse Nationals capture the 1955 NBA championship. Jerry Sloan grew up on a farm in southern Illinois. He got up at 4:30 A.M. to do chores. Then he walked two miles (3.2 km) to school for 7:00 A.M. practice. The Baltimore Bullets chose him fourth in the 1965 NBA Draft. They traded him to Chicago the following year as the Bulls joined the expanding NBA.

Forward **TERRY DISCHINGER** stayed with the Zephyrs when the team moved to Baltimore.

stayed away. Changing their name to the Zephyrs didn't help. They lost 55 games. Chicago businessman Dick Klein wanted to buy the team and keep it in Chicago. He couldn't. The Zephyrs moved to Baltimore. Klein didn't give up. He asked the NBA for an expansion team. The league agreed. He paid $1.6 million in 1966 for his franchise. His family thought up the nickname in his living room. His son Greg recalled, "We knew we had this new team and we'd be playing in the International Amphitheater near the stockyards," he said. "We were throwing around one-syllable names to fit in with the Cubs, Sox, Bears.... But the best I can recall us coming up with was Steers. Then my younger brother Mark came into the room with one of his favorite children's books, *The Story of Ferdinand*." Bulls it was. They are strong animals with a never-say-die attitude.

During their first year in the league, the Bulls faced the St. Louis Hawks in the playoffs.

T he Bulls lived up to their name right away. It was the start of the 1966–67 season. Chicago played the St. Louis Hawks. Hawks player/coach Richie Guerin said the Bulls would be lucky to win 10 games. The Bulls made him eat his words. They won that night and three of their next four games. "I thought, 'My goodness, we're not that good, are we?'" said forward/guard Jerry Sloan before the next game. "We certainly found out that night. The Knicks waxed us pretty good, and reality started to set in." Chicago sank to last place by the end of February. On March 1, the Bulls hosted the Philadelphia 76ers. The Sixers would win 68 regular-season games and the championship. Somehow, the Bulls posted a 129–122 victory. That spurred Chicago to win 7 of its final 11 games. The Bulls qualified for the playoffs. No expansion team had ever made the playoffs in its first year. It hasn't happened since. St. Louis swept the Bulls in the first round. But Bulls coach Johnny Kerr was voted NBA Coach of the Year.

MJ ARRIVES

The Bulls had losing records for the next three years. They squeezed into the playoffs twice. Both times they lost in the first round. In 1970–71, third-year coach Dick Motta led Chicago to a 51–31 mark. The team surpassed the 50-win mark the next three years as well. Led by Sloan and scrappy guard Norm Van Lier,

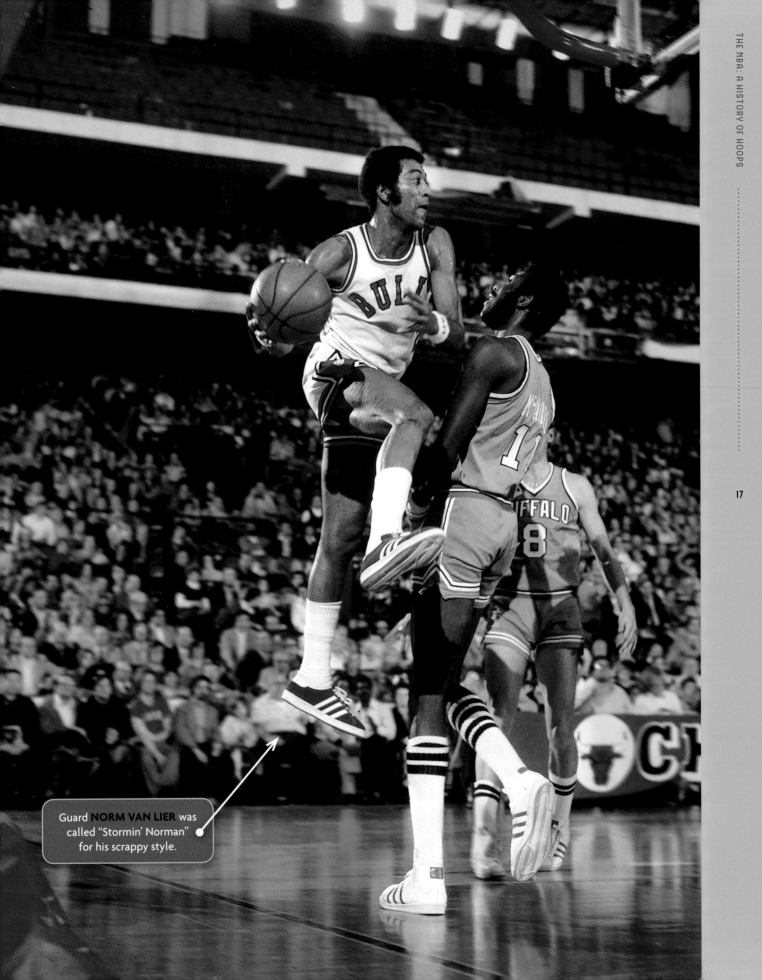

Guard **NORM VAN LIER** was called "Stormin' Norman" for his scrappy style.

The Bulls battled the Lakers in the 1971 conference semifinals, ultimately losing.

Chicago developed a reputation for tough defense. "Playing the Bulls is like running through a barbed wire fence," said Los Angeles Lakers guard Gail Goodrich. "You may win the game, but they're gonna put lumps on you." The Bulls advanced to the conference finals in 1974 and 1975. Both times they could go no further. When Chicago dropped to 24 wins in 1975–76, Motta was fired. After a brief revival keyed by 7-foot-2 center Artis Gilmore, the Bulls plunged to 31 wins in 1978–79. They were just as

19

LEGENDS OF THE HARDWOOD

ALMOST MAKING MAGIC

The Bulls had the worst record in the Western Conference in 1978–79. That gave them a 50/50 chance of drafting future Hall-of-Famer Earvin "Magic" Johnson. They flipped a coin with Los Angeles for the first pick. The Bulls called heads. It was tails. With the second pick, Chicago chose UCLA star David Greenwood. The forward/center averaged 12.6 points a game in 6 seasons. In losing, Chicago may also have won. "Nothing against Greenwood, who was a good player and a good guy," said longtime Bulls official Irwin Mandel. "But with Magic, we never would have had a bad enough record to draft [Michael] Jordan five seasons later."

At 7-foot-2, **ARTIS "A-TRAIN" GILMORE** kept opponents away from the basket.

bad the following year. The Bulls rebounded to win 45 games and reach the second round of the playoffs in 1980–81. Yet they fell back to 34–48 the following season. They traded Gilmore. The result was obvious. "Lack of a dominating center is the major reason [the Bulls] have lost 111 games in the last 2 seasons," wrote the *Chicago Tribune* before the 1984 NBA Draft.

C hicago wanted a big man to replace Gilmore. Houston had the first pick. The Rockets took center Hakeem "The Dream" Olajuwon. Portland drafted second. The Trail Blazers chose 7-foot-1 shot blocker and rebounder Sam Bowie. Rod Thorn, Chicago's general manager, was disappointed. Chicago had the third pick. Thorn tried to trade that pick for an established center. He couldn't swing a deal. Somewhat reluctantly, he chose guard Michael Jordan. "We wish he

Boosted by star guard **MICHAEL "AIR" JORDAN**, the Bulls began to soar.

were seven feet tall, but he isn't," Thorn said. "There just wasn't a center available. What can you do?" It didn't take long for Jordan to show what he could do. The Bulls finished just 38–44 and lost in the first round of the playoffs. But Jordan was Rookie of the Year. Soon he earned the nickname "Air Jordan." He could remain airborne longer than anyone else.

Despite having losing records the next two years, the Bulls made the playoffs both times. And both times they were swept in three games. Jordan scored 63 points against the Boston Celtics in 1986. It was a playoff record. The following season, he became the second player in NBA history to score 3,000 points in a season. He also proved to be more than just a scoring machine. He was the first NBA player to get 200 steals and 100 blocks. By then he had help. Chicago added rugged forward Charles Oakley in 1985.

LEGENDS OF THE HARDWOOD

NOW BATTING ...
MICHAEL JORDAN

Michael Jordan's father was murdered in 1993. Soon after, Jordan stunned the basketball world by retiring to play professional baseball. "It began as my father's idea," Jordan said. "We had seen Bo Jackson and Deion Sanders try two sports, and my father had said that he felt I could have made it in baseball, too." Jordan joined the Class AA Birmingham Barons in 1994. But there was one problem. "Baseball is a function of repetition," said Texas Rangers batting coach Tom House. Jordan's new teammates had been swinging bats while Jordan was shooting baskets. He wound up hitting just .202 with the Barons. He left baseball and rejoined the Bulls.

THREE-PEAT

The Bulls hit their stride in 1987–88, winning 50 games. The league named Jordan Most Valuable Player (MVP), Defensive Player of the Year, and All-Star Game MVP. The Bulls crafted one of their most productive drafts. They added power forward Horace Grant. They also traded their number-eight pick, center

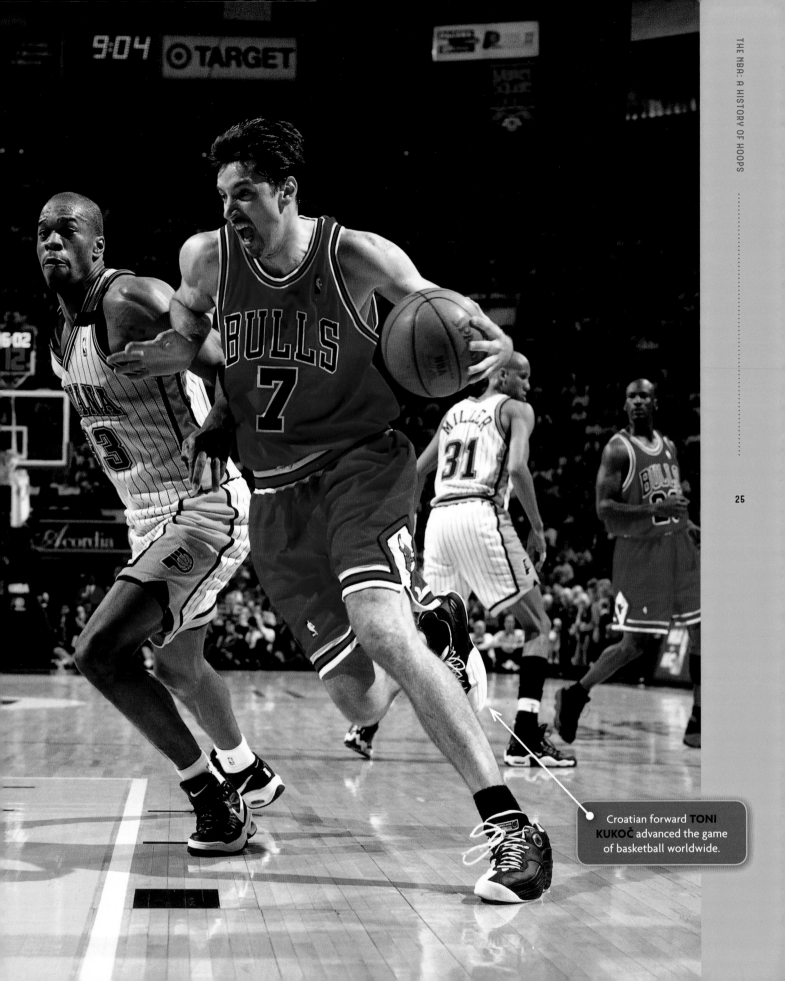

Croatian forward **TONI KUKOČ** advanced the game of basketball worldwide.

Seven-time All-Star **SCOTTIE PIPPEN** later had his jersey retired by the Bulls.

"THEY GOT IN OUR HEAD WITH THE
PHYSICAL STUFF," PIPPEN SAID OF THE
THREE EARLIER PLAYOFF DEFEATS. "BUT
IN DOING IT, THE PISTONS TAUGHT US
THE TOUGHNESS WE NEEDED."

Olden Polynice, to Seattle. The Sonics had used their fifth pick to take forward Scottie Pippen. He then joined the Bulls. "I never heard of him or his school [the University of Central Arkansas]," Jordan said of Pippen. But soon the entire country knew Pippen's name. He became a full-time starter in the playoffs that year. The Bulls, though, lost to the Detroit Pistons. The Pistons were known as the "Bad Boys" for their aggressive playing style. Chicago lost to the Pistons in the playoffs again the following year.

Phil Jackson stepped in as coach in 1989. He guided the team to a 55–27 mark. Once again, Chicago couldn't get past the Pistons in the Eastern Conference finals. Three years of frustration ended the following year. After winning an NBA-best 61 games, the Bulls swept Detroit in the conference finals. "They got in our head with the physical stuff," Pippen said of the three earlier playoff defeats. "But in doing it, the Pistons taught us the toughness we needed." Jordan and Pippen steered the Bulls past the Los Angeles Lakers to claim their first NBA title. The Bulls were even better the following season. Their 67 wins were the best in team history. They stomped over Portland in the Finals. In 1992–93, Jordan won his seventh scoring title in a row. B. J. Armstrong moved into the starting lineup. He led the NBA in three-point percentage at .453. Many people thought the Phoenix Suns would win the NBA title. The Bulls didn't. They defeated the Suns in six games. Winning three titles in a row became

Point guard **B. J. ARMSTRONG** specialized in shooting from the three-point range.

known as a "three-peat." The Bulls' three-peat was the first since the Boston Celtics' string of eight straight championships between 1959 and 1966.

Many fans thought that Chicago could win four titles in a row. They were stunned when Jordan announced his retirement before the start of the 1993–94 season. He was just 30 and obviously at the peak of his game. He wanted to play professional baseball. Chicago still won 55 games without him. But the Bulls lost to the New York Knicks in the second playoff round.

LEGENDS OF THE HARDWOOD

NUMBERS GAME

Michael Jordan's high school basketball number was 45. But on varsity, his older brother already wore number 45. Jordan divided 45 by 2 and rounded up to 23. It became the NBA's most famous number. He returned to the Bulls near the end of the 1994–95 season, wearing number 45. "I thought of my return as a new beginning," he wrote. That "new beginning" ended quickly. In the playoffs, Orlando Magic guard Nick Anderson stole the ball from Jordan in the final seconds. The Magic won. "No. 45 doesn't explode like No. 23 used to," Anderson bragged. The criticism stung. The Bulls had retired number 23. But Jordan wore it for the rest of his career in Chicago.

An elite defender, **DENNIS RODMAN** averaged 15.3 rebounds per game with Chicago.

AND ANOTHER ONE

Jordan soon realized he had no future in baseball. With the Bulls struggling, Jordan returned late in the 1994–95 season. He helped the Bulls advance to the Eastern Conference semifinals. But the Bulls bowed

The Bulls overcame the Utah Jazz in the 1998 NBA Finals to clinch their second three-peat.

32

out to the Orlando Magic in six games. Some people said that Jordan wasn't as good as he had been. Jordan wanted to prove them wrong. He trained especially hard for the following season. He received help from an unexpected direction. Former Detroit "Bad Boy" Dennis Rodman joined the team. His fierce defense and rebounding helped the Bulls win an all-time NBA-best 72 games. "The 1995–96 Chicago Bulls won 72 in large part because Michael Jordan made it a priority to break the previous record for most wins in a season," said basketball writer Diamond Leung. The Bulls beat the Seattle Sonics in four games to win their fourth NBA title.

Chicago won 69 games the following season and repeated as NBA champions. The Bulls stood on the verge of history as the 1997–98 season began. No team had ever won three straight championships twice. Though Chicago won "only" 62 regular-season games, it advanced to the NBA Finals. The Bulls took a three-games-to-two lead over the Utah Jazz. In the final moments of Game 6, the Jazz led by three points. If Utah won, the final game would be played on its home court. Jordan scored to narrow Utah's margin to a single point. Then he stripped the ball from Karl Malone. "We all knew what was coming next," said basketball writer Mitchel Lawrence. "It was just a matter of how Jordan would do it. Working against Byron Russell, his stutter-step move sent

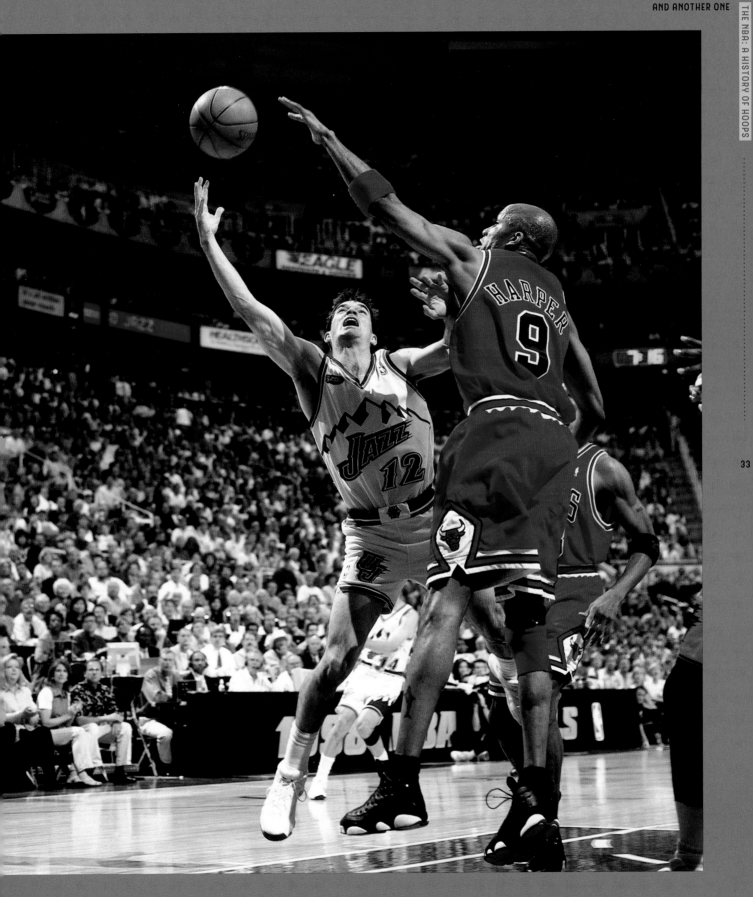

BUGS BUNNY

MICHAEL JORDAN

34

STARRING MICHAEL JORDAN

Michael Jordan went Hollywood in 1996. He starred in the movie *Space Jam*. In the movie, an amusement park owner wants a new attraction. He thinks Looney Tunes characters such as Bugs Bunny, Daffy Duck, and Elmer Fudd would be perfect. He sends his small helpers to kidnap them. The Looney Tunes squad challenges them to a basketball game to keep their freedom. Bugs Bunny asks Jordan to help the Looney Tunes win the game. Film critic Gene Siskel liked Jordan's performance. "He wisely accepted as a first movie a script that builds nicely on his genial personality," Siskel wrote.

the Jazz defender to the floor, allowing Jordan to get an open jumper with 5.2 seconds left. Hello, title No. 6." It was Jordan's last basket as a Bulls player. He announced his retirement soon afterward. Many people consider him the greatest basketball player in history. Certainly he is the most famous.

Jordan wasn't the only missing face when the Bulls opened the 1998–99 season. Coach Jackson also left. The team traded Pippen and released Rodman. In addition, the team's draft picks during the 1990s generally didn't turn out well. The Bulls had no replacements for their stars. The team plummeted to 13–37 in the strike-shortened 1998–99 season. Toni Kukoč was one bright spot. He led the team in scoring, rebounds, and assists. Chicago traded him when the season ended. Swingman Elton Brand shared Rookie of the Year honors in 1999–2000, but the team finished 17–65. Chicago did even worse the following year. They played seven rookies and stumbled to a franchise-worst 15–67. The next three years weren't much better. Sometimes non-basketball issues arose. The Bulls drafted point guard Jay Williams with the second overall pick in 2002. After a good rookie season, Williams crashed his motorcycle into a lamppost. His injuries ended his NBA career.

36

STAMPEDING AGAIN

Under coach Scott Skiles, the Bulls turned things around in 2004–05. Their 47 victories more than doubled the total from the previous year. One key was the play of second-year

Point guard **KIRK HINRICH** became a leader on the court and behind the scenes.

When he was healthy, lightning-fast **DERRICK ROSE** rarely took a seat on the bench.

THIBODEAU GUIDED THE BULLS TO THE TOP SPOT IN THE EASTERN CONFERENCE IN 2010–11. CHICAGO WON 62 GAMES. THAT TIED THE RECORD FOR A ROOKIE COACH.

point guard Kirk Hinrich. He and shifty shooting guard Ben Gordon gave Chicago one of the league's best backcourts. The improved play of small forward Luol Deng helped propel Chicago to the 2006–07 Eastern Conference semifinals. The Bulls lost to Detroit, four games to two. The team got off to a bad start the following year. Skiles was fired. The Bulls stumbled to a 33–49 record. That dismal mark had one consolation.

Chicago gained the top pick in the 2008 NBA Draft. The Bulls chose point guard Derrick Rose. He was voted Rookie of the Year. After two straight 41–41 seasons, Chicago hired defensive specialist Tom Thibodeau as coach. It was his first head coaching job. Thibodeau guided the Bulls to the top spot in the Eastern Conference in 2010–11. Chicago won 62 games. That tied the record for a rookie coach. Rose was named MVP. He was the youngest player to win the award. But LeBron James and the Miami Heat burned Chicago in five games in the conference finals.

40

KEEPING FANS ENTERTAINED

During breaks in the game, Chicago fans enjoy a variety of entertainment. Team mascot Benny the Bull soars above the rim for breathtaking dunks. The Chicago Bulls Bucket Boys beat rhythms on plastic buckets. The Luvabulls perform dance routines. The Junior Luvabulls is for girls aged 5 to 17. BullsKidz are a dozen youngsters between the ages of 7 and 12. They perform hip-hop and jazz moves at many weekend home games. For nearly a decade starting in 2003, the Matadors were a fan favorite. The Matadors were a team of about a dozen big—sometimes REALLY big—men. Their main mission was to make people laugh.

ROSE racked up an average of 25 points per game in 2010–11.

41

A players' strike shortened the following season. Chicago still won 50 games. The Bulls had high hopes for the playoffs. But Rose suffered a serious knee injury in the first round, and Chicago lost to the 76ers. Rose missed the entire 2012–13 season. The Bulls still won 45 games and advanced to the second round of the playoffs. With Rose playing just 10 games, the Bulls made the playoffs again in 2013–14, but lost in the first round. Things looked better in 2014–15. Small forward Jimmy Butler was

Power forward **NIKOLA MIROTIC** honed his shooting skills in 2015–16, his second Chicago season.

Forward **DOUG McDERMOTT** showed potential for being an offensive threat early on.

THINGS LOOKED BETTER IN 2014–15. SMALL FORWARD JIMMY BUTLER WAS NAMED THE NBA'S MOST IMPROVED PLAYER. CENTER JOAKIM NOAH, 2014 DEFENSIVE PLAYER OF THE YEAR, ANCHORED THE MIDDLE. CHICAGO WON 50 GAMES.

named the NBA's Most Improved Player. Center Joakim Noah, 2014 Defensive Player of the Year, anchored the middle. Chicago won 50 games. But it lost to the Cleveland Cavaliers in the Eastern Conference semifinals. Rose began the 2015–16 season with another injury—a fractured cheekbone. The Bulls finished with 42 wins and missed the playoffs. They quickly signed Miami Heat superstar guard Dwyane Wade in free agency. Wade grew up in Chicago. In 2016–17, the Bulls managed only a 41–41 mark. Wade's average of 18.3 points per game was his lowest since his rookie season. But with point guard Rajon Rondo playing a key role by season's end, Chicago beat the Celtics in the first two playoff games in Boston. After Rondo broke his thumb, though, the Celtics rallied to take the next four games.

During their five decades, the Chicago Bulls have had their ups and downs. Those ups have been among the NBA's greatest moments. Fans hope that the new generation of young stars—along with the veteran presence of Wade—can rise to the same heights. Nothing would make them happier than a third three-peat.

SELECTED BIBLIOGRAPHY

Ballard, Chris. *The Art of a Beautiful Game: The Thinking Fan's Tour of the NBA*. New York: Simon & Schuster, 2010.

Hubbard, Jan, ed. *The Official NBA Basketball Encyclopedia*. 3rd edition. New York: Doubleday, 2000.

Lazenby, Roland. *Michael Jordan: The Life*. New York: Little, Brown, 2014.

NBA.com. "Chicago Bulls." http://www.nba.com/bulls/.

Simmons, Bill. *The Book of Basketball: The NBA According to the Sports Guy*. New York: Ballantine, 2009.

Sports Illustrated. *Sports Illustrated Basketball's Greatest*. New York: Sports Illustrated, 2014.

WEBSITES

DUCKSTERS BASKETBALL: NBA

http://www.ducksters.com/sports/national_basketball_association.php

Learn more about NBA history, rules, positions, strategy, drills, and other topics.

JR. NBA

http://jr.nba.com/

This kids site has games, videos, game results, team and player information, statistics, and more.

Note: Every effort has been made to ensure that any websites listed above were active at the time of publication. However, because of the nature of the Internet, it is impossible to guarantee that these sites will remain active indefinitely or that their contents will not be altered.

INDEX